GARY HOFFMAN

DOGS ON THE TRAIL

Hiking, Camping, and Traveling With Your Dog

InsightOut Publishing

Greenfield, Wisconsin

Dogs on the Trail

Hiking, Camping and Traveling with Your Dog
by Gary Hoffman

ISBN 0-9769943-0-5

Cover and interior design by Bookcovers.com
Illustrations by Woodie Hoffman
Cover Photo by Barry Borne

TABLE OF CONTENTS

ACKNOWLEDGEMENTS

As with any book or project, nothing is a one-person show. I'd like to thank my wife for putting up with me through the long process of compiling and writing this book as well as for her wonderful cartoons and illustrations.

Thanks to my good friend and pro photographer Barry Borne for the great shot of me and my flat-coat Audi and for all of his help in sorting out this book to read well.

Thanks to Dave Musikof, president of the California Canine Hikers, for his suggestions, guidance and never ending support.

Thanks to Michael Grant for all of his expertise in computer skills as well as his willingness and guidance in this project.

I'm sure I've forgotten other people that played a part in putting this book together as well. Forgive me if I did not mention you, but you are all appreciated.

Most of all, thanks to all of my readers for their compliments of my previous books and encouragement and suggestions for this book. I hope I've made your outings with your dogs a bit more fun and a lot safer.

See you on the trail!

Gary Hoffman

INTRODUCTION

In my youth, I was confident that my dog and I would be fine on any hiking, camping or backpacking trip. I was fairly well organized and certain that I had the necessary equipment and knowledge to be in the wilderness. And after all, my dog should be right at home!

There were a few hikers that had their dogs with them, and when our paths did cross, most were friendly and happy to share a story or two. While our dogs would be busy with their greeting rituals, their owners' stories seemed to have the same theme. They were unprepared for weather conditions, insects or injuries. Their dogs were eating backpacking and junk food and often had stomach problems. Some dogs had torn pads and were ragged looking and often out of control or just looked tired and sick.

I decided that perhaps luck had played a large part with my successful trips and I needed to further my knowledge of the outdoors and first aid for me, and for my dog as well.

I started attending backpacking seminars and reading every book I could find on any related subject. I became aware of all the potential hazards of heading off into the wilderness without the proper equipment or knowledge to handle all the perils that seemed to happen to a fair share of people. Though I still believe the wilderness is safer than any city, when disaster strikes in the middle of nowhere, I had better be able to handle it myself. A lot of the information I learned carried over to dogs, but there were still a slew of questions I had about bringing my four-footed friend with me.

Before I wrote my first book, *Happy Trails For You And Your Dog* the only book that existed on backpacking with dogs, was an out of print book last published in 1979 by Alan and Joan Riley called "Taking Your Dog Backpacking". It took me nearly a year to locate a copy. Books on Hunting Dogs were helpful, but there simply wasn't enough information about hiking and backpacking and all the perils of being deep in the wilderness with a dog. Some of the first-aid and backpacking seminar information could be utilized for dogs, so I did the best I could at preparing my dogs the same way I prepared myself for any camping trip or long hike. There were books on veterinary first-aid, but too many sections ended with "take your dog to the vet". Sound information, but impractical when we were days away from civilization.

Since then, there has been a huge increase of people interested in taking their dogs with them camping, hiking and backpacking. My publisher and I agreed that my previous book *Hiking With Your Dog* needed to be updated and expanded. We had received a great deal of input over the years and I asked all the people I knew who hike with their dogs and have read my book, what they would like to see in a new book. Most said they wanted more on travel, day hikes and camping. Not only information on backpacking. Many people said they would like to see more information about first aid and training. I hope I have succeeded in covering these topics in a clear and cohesive fashion. My first-aid information has come to me from several veterinarians, as well as some of the veterinary books I own. My training information also came from asking trainers who handle dogs for hunting or mushing and reading every dog training book I could get my hands on.

People such as Dave Musikof, the president of the California Canine Hikers, was very concerned with the lack of trail etiquette and irresponsible dog owners that he had seen over his many years of hiking.

Park rangers have told me about endless reports of loose dogs bothering or even terrorizing other campers and their dogs. They also told me about dog feces left unburied or not packed out and barking dogs disturbing people's peace day and night.

Dogs were disturbing wildlife and possibly destroying the frail chance of survival that truly wild animals have. This has led to the exclusion of dogs in many parks and wilderness areas. Unless each one of us considers ourselves a representative of how a well-behaved dog does not detract from other people's peace, the closures will only increase.

I have a website www.dogsonthetrail.com for all of us to share our experiences, evaluate new equipment and keep everyone up to date on new first aid techniques and training advice. I will also have a newsletter so the latest information can be sent right to your computer.

I hope you will enjoy this book and share your comments, questions and suggestions so that we might all benefit from each other's experiences.

Happy Trails!

Chapter

SELECTING A DOG

I f you haven't picked out a dog yet, the first question should be why do you want a dog? Play devil's advocate and examine your motives. Will your lifestyle accommodate having a pet for the next decade or more?

The next question should be, what type of dog do I want? And the answer should not be based on how cute this particular breed is, but should be based on your work schedule, lifestyle, activity level and time you will have to properly train and exercise your new dog.

Are you an active person? Do you mind getting up every morning and taking your dog for a long walk? Do you have small children? Can you give your Border Collie a good three-hour workout, at least twice a day? If not, then a Border Collie or herding type dog should not be on your list. They are cute and they are smart as a whip, but they were bred to herd and to be very active working dogs. If you can't tire this dog out, you will have a potentially very bad animal on your hands.

Any dog can be your traveling companion as well as your hiking companion. Some breeds may be better suited for different weather or more difficult hikes or backpacks, but any dog can be wonderful company and should add to, not distract, from your outdoor adventures.

There are some breeds that have a much harder time than others. Breeds with short muzzles can have chronic breathing problems. Breeds with extremely heavy bone structure can have lower energy and less endurance.

Talk to your vet, or a trainer, the Humane Society or check out some of the websites that talk about choosing a dog. Matching the right dog for the right family is the start of a great relationship. Daniel F. Tortora wrote a book titled, *The Right Dog For You* that is extremely helpful in choosing a new dog.

I'd also like to emphasize the amount of work it is to raise a puppy. It pays off in the end, if you truly have the time, but a puppy can be as much work as a new baby. It seems that nature made all puppies cute so they would all get adopted, but many people find they aren't so cute when they have chewed your furniture and stained your carpet for the umpteenth time. Of course in the correct situation, with educated owners that have the time, desire and the knowledge, the results are wonderful and the effort well worth it.

There are also many wonderful dogs wait-

ing for adoption that are past all those ter-
rible puppy stages and only require the
knowledge and time to get used to a new
family and adapt to your way of life. No dog
is ever too old to learn. Old habits may be
hard to break, but when the desired action is
rewarded and the undesired action ignored, it
won't take long for your dog to figure out
which is the best choice.

There are many adult dogs that end up for
adoption for a multitude of reasons, and it's
rare that the problem is actually the dog.

If he was a street dog, chances are he is not
used to the sounds of a hair dryer, or a gar-
bage disposal. Being indoors may make him
anxious. It's quite the culture shock to a street
dog. Nothing is familiar. He has entered your
home with his own set of baggage. Leashes
and newspapers may have a different meaning
to him. Commands such as come and stay or
down, may bring a reaction you did not expect.
Most of the behavior problems you may encounter are usually from the demands of your
lifestyle or bad habits instilled from the last
owner. Successful training may go very slow in
the beginning, but if you're patient and com-
mitted, you will eventually get good results. It
typically takes six to twelve weeks before a

new dog is adjusted to your home. A large dose of obedience, patience, attention and positive re-enforcement will go a long way to having your dog adjust to his new home and lifestyle.

Don't Shoot The Dog by Karen Pryor is hailed as one of the best books ever written on understanding dogs and gives great insight into raising a dog. It's been on my bookshelf for years as it's usually one of the first books I loan to friends who have a new dog. It's a fun read and extremely informative. *The Culture Clash* by Jean Donaldson has taught me more about understanding canines than any book I've read. These two books will make selecting a dog and training him easier because you will understand how a dog thinks. We tend to project our human emotions onto our dogs and we are not dealing with humans here. I can't praise these two books enough.

My dogs have all been from shelters except for my current puppy, Willy. He came from a litter that an acquaintance of ours told us about. Our children are grown and out of the house and my wife wanted a little dog this time. This little guy came from a litter of a purebred Pomeranian male and a Chihuahua mix female. All the pups came out looking like Pomeranian mixes, but this little guy looks like a scruffy little Yorkshire terrier mix! He is best described as "Disney cute". It is possible for a mother to carry pups from more than one male. My guess is Willy's mom had a secret fling!

It's been a long time since I've raised a puppy and for all I thought I knew, I am still amazed as to how much work and attention is needed. He is ten months old as of this writing and is settling down a bit and is turning out to be a joy.

I still plan on adopting a larger breed for the kind of hiking I like to do. Dogs that fit in with my lifestyle are not ultra high-energy dogs. I'm no longer young, though I still do a fair share of hiking. I like a dog that will mellow out in front of the fire all day if I desire, or hike all day or all week should I so desire. There are several breeds that fit into this category, but my particular favorites are retrievers and labs. The best hiking dog I've ever owned was a flat-coat retriever that I named Audi. My son was born deaf and I had my hands quite full taking care of him, so when I went to the local shelter, I was looking for a dog that was past the difficult puppy stage, but still young enough that I could train her and hike with her for many years. As I strolled past all the dogs, they all barked and jumped and were hoping I'd be the one to spring them. I wished I could have taken them all home. As I walked past one cage, a medium size black dog just sat there and looked at me with her sad eyes and did not bark at all. I backed up to take another look. She looked to be about one year old. She had long silky black hair, healthy white teeth and beautiful bright brown eyes. I asked her to come to me and she did. I asked her to sit and she sat. I asked for her paw and she immediately raised her paw and smiled as retrievers do. I knew this was my new friend. With no information on her past, I had to ask myself how a wonderful dog like this ended up in a shelter. Perhaps she ran away? I doubted that, as she was obviously well groomed and showed no signs of abuse. Perhaps someone died or moved some place where they couldn't have a dog? Often times young couples get a dog and then when they get pregnant they figure having a baby and a dog will be too much for them. There are endless scenarios as to how this fantastic dog may have ended up in a shelter, but I feel when fate hands you a gift, it's best to gratefully accept. I would never know the reason she ended up in a shelter, but I would like to think that I was meant to be her owner.

I had already picked out her name, Audi, which was short for Audio. Since my son is deaf, I knew this dog was going to have to learn hand signals. I knew retrievers were very sight oriented as they were bred to be hunting dogs. She learned hand signals in no time and when teaching her new tricks, she often learned the hand signal faster than the verbal command. She was a perfect match for me and for my family.

Flat-coats are typically happy-go-lucky dogs with great dispositions. Very much like Golden Retrievers. Ready to go at a moments notice yet happy just to be lying around with the family. She was easy to train and turned out to be the best hiking buddy and companion that I ever could have hoped for.

A few years later my life got more compli-cated and I thought it might be a good idea to get another dog and perhaps they could keep each other company when I couldn't be there. I have seen this work out for other people, but in my case, I just ended up with two dogs vying for my attention. They liked each other, or maybe only tolerated each other, but they sure never played together. Sadie was a Sheltie mix I found in a different shelter. I knew she would be a high-energy dog, but I was quite certain then, that between my attention and my growing family, as well as Audi, she would be kept quite busy. For the most part that turned out to be true, but I always felt that I could not give either one the full attention they required or deserved.

They both went on to be great hiking dogs and lived very long and full lives. My pups both lived to about fifteen years. It's hard to think ahead that far, but it's quite important to try to project what your life may be like not only in fifteen years, but during those years as well.

Do you like to fly all over the world? Does your job take you away a great deal of the time? Do you spend a great deal of time at your job? How long will your dog be home alone every day? Do you have babies, or plan to have babies? Some dogs are one-person dogs and very protective. They can get jealous of babies, children or anyone else.

These and many other factors should go into the decision of not just what breed of dog to get, but whether or not a dog will fit into your life for the next decade or more. If you start out with a puppy, you have a better chance of socializing your dog to children, dogs, cats or anything and everything you may encounter in your life. The socialization window is really from three to five months. After that, it is not impossible, but much more work and patience will be necessary to improve socialization skills.

I also recommend Carol Lea Benjamin's book, *Second Hand Dog as* a "must have" for anyone adopting a dog. It is informative and also a fun read.

Selecting the right dog for you and your lifestyle is the first step to having an enjoyable relationship. Learning what to expect and how to accomplish it is the next.

Chapter 2

TRAVEL

Teaching your dog to be a good traveler is essential for any successful outing. Learning to travel safely will ensure many happy trails.

Dogs can be great travelers. They are always eager to go with you wherever and whenever you wish. But if all their car trips are to the vet, groomer, or someplace unpleasant for them, then riding in the car will quickly be associated as something bad.

Some dogs just take more time getting used to riding in moving vehicles. They may not have had bad experiences, but just have a problem with the motion and all the sounds, sights and smells that are whizzing past them.

First, I'd like to discuss car and truck safety devices for your dog. Just because we used to toss the dog in the car or tie him to a rope in the back of the truck and nothing bad ever happened, doesn't mean that it never will. If your dog is not belted in with the proper harness, he becomes a projectile should you get in an accident or have to slam on the brakes or make a quick maneuver.

I had the horrible experience of actually witnessing a dog that was simply roped to the inside of a pickup truck and was hurled out along side the truck without the driver being aware. I'll spare you the gory details. I sped up to catch the unaware driver and he immediately pulled over. We wrapped his dog in a blanket he had and I gave him directions to the nearest vet. He may have been a good guy and loved his pet as much as anyone, but his ignorance or laziness could have cost his dog his life or mobility and the nightmares of having been the person that injured his cherished pet.

Had his dog been wearing a simple harness, and been tied off properly (see diagram) this never would have happened. It takes me thirty seconds to put the harness on my dog, and about twenty seconds more to clip him in properly. Either leave a minute or two earlier or don't take your dog!

Too many people simply have their dog jump
in their car and roam about while they drive.
My pet peeve (pardon the pun) is when people
have their dog is in their lap and face while
they are driving! I was smarter than that when
I was sixteen, and we did some dumb things!
They wouldn't have their child roam about, or
their teenager sit in their lap, but somehow it's
ok if it's a dog.

In my opinion the best product on the market is the award winning harness made by
Ruff Rider, called "The Roadie" It was designed with the help of a veterinary orthope-
dic surgeon. I use it on my dog even if we are
going one block. It is made with the dogs'

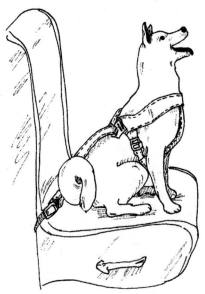

safety and comfort in mind. It takes all of thirty seconds to put on and my dog has come to love it because he knows it means we are "going for a ride". Check out www.ruffrider.com for more information. This product came into being because of the personal experience of the company's creator, Carl Goldberg. That story and how "The Roadie" was developed, is on his website. If you don't like using computers, give them a call at Ruff Rider Products Inc. 720-249-2986.

Please remember, loose objects e.g. your dog, is a projectile if not harnessed properly. In an auto accident, a 60 pound dog in a car traveling 30 mph will hit an object ten inches in front of him / her at 1,200 pounds per square inch.

Animal safety is finally becoming a concern in our country. There are more than twenty-seven statutes in twenty-five U.S. states that have laws protecting animals being transported. California, New Hampshire, Massachusetts, Maine, Oregon, Washington and Rhode Island have restricted dogs from pick-up trucks or open vehicles with the exception of some working dogs.

Many people are under the impression that dogs are safe in crates in their vehicles, when they are no safer than your baby or child would be in a crate. Plus the crate itself can come flying at you in an accident. A high quality car restraint is fast, easy and safe. It's the only way to go!

If your dog is afraid of riding in the car or has motion sickness, the best way to get him used to riding in vehicles is to break him in very slowly. If you are sure it is motion sickness, your vet can treat him with meclizine, or other medication for dogs. In almost all cases you can get your dog used to traveling by taking very short trips and rewarding him for being good. Even if it is up and down the driveway to begin with, at least the car will be associated with something positive. Once you've done the driveway bit a few times, move up to going around the block. Make sure you don't act like you are dreading this. Get the harness and ask him if he wants to go for a ride, making "ride" sound like a fun thing. It should be! And it will be! Smile, get excited, put on his harness and give him a treat. Belt him in and praise him or give him a treat for being such a good dog. When you come back home, give him another treat and tell him what a good dog he's been. Eventually move on to longer trips. Soon, riding in the car will equate to fun. Weaning him off of treats is not a difficult task. Some dogs work for praise easily and some need more coaxing. All the trainers that I know feel that treats are a great motivator and are easily discontinued.

Allowing your dog to have his head or nose out the window means that he's probably not belted in correctly, and it is also a bad idea because grit often gets in their eyes and nose. The wind can also cause inflammation of the ears and throat.

Once you have advanced to long trips, remember that you should stop at least every two hours and give your dog a chance to have a drink, and to walk around and relieve himself. Ditto for yourself! Make sure you bring his bowl, purified water, and be sure he is leashed when letting him out of the car. Trucks and cars rushing by easily spook dogs, or they are so anxious to get out that they rush right onto the road. Always exit curbside with dog on leash, leash in hand.

If it is particularly hot in the car, offer your dog ice cubes or ice shavings. And please, if you need to stop and leave your dog in the car on a warm day, make sure there is plenty of ventilation and park in the shade. Leaving your dog in the car on a hot day, even for a couple of minutes, can be deadly. Every year we hear stories about people who have done this to their pets. It almost always takes longer to run in the store and pick up that item, or take care of business, than you think it will. Better to leave your pup at home than to risk overheating him. It only takes a couple of minutes to cause heat stroke.

If you are planning a long trip, call ahead or get on the computer and find out where pets are accepted and plan your trip accordingly. One good site is www.dogfriendly.com/.

If people continue to abuse the rules of hotels and motels, fewer establishments will accept pets. The same goes for waysides and rest stops. If we are conscientious about cleaning up the mess our pets make and not allowing them to bark and disturb other people, dogs will be welcome at more locations.

This is probably a good place to mention bringing along your dogs license and proof of vaccination when traveling. Proper papers are required if you are traveling out of state or country. Every dog should have some sort of ID / identification tag. Many shelters and vets offer microchips that are painlessly implanted and are on file with a national registry. There are also tattoos that insure your dog can never lose his ID, but even with the use of microchips or tattoos, I still believe that having standard identification on his collar is the best place. It takes a special scanner to read the microchips and tattoos are often overlooked. An ID tag will be recognized by anyone who finds your dog and will easily be understood. Make sure you put his name, address and the best phone number(s) for reaching you. This would obviously be your cellular phone number when traveling. I like to put two phone numbers on my dog's tags, plus the offer of a reward.

Chapter 3

EQUIPMENT

M ost people do not hesitate to bring a slew of goodies along to make themselves more comfortable, but when it comes to their dogs, often it's the bare minimum or nothing at all. This is part of the misconception that dogs are wild animals and will therefore be right at home in the wilderness or outdoors. Here is a quote from *A Potpourri of Pooches,* by Peter Tyson.

> *"Dogs would never have become so diversified without our, well, dogged manipulation of canine mating. It's not known exactly when people and pups first got together, but it was a long time ago. The first archeological evidence of dogs morphologically distinct from wolves comes from roughly 12,000 years ago in the Middle East. By that time and perhaps much earlier—Wayne's genetic data hint that dogs split from wolves about 135,000 years ago—dogs appear to have been at least semi-domesticated. By 2000 B.C., dogs resembling the modern Pharaoh hound are depicted on Egyptian tombs, implying that both domestication and diversification were well under way."*

That being said, it is evident our dogs are hardly "wild animals" anymore and should require at the very least, the things that make them as comfortable as they are at home.

We bring sleeping bags, ground pads, wind and rain gear, boots, gloves, hats, food, drink and treats for ourselves and often, much more. Dogs that have spent their lives indoors need warmth, protection from weather conditions, their regular food and treats, and perhaps a favorite toy or two.

For serious backpacks, it will take a well-trained and conditioned dog to be able to carry all the items they will need. I will go into further detail in future chapters. Car camping has very little limitations as to the amount of goodies you can bring. There is no reason why you and your dog can't be just about as comfortable as you would be at home.

In all instances, day hikes, car camping, or backpacks, I always carry a pack with at least, the minimum essentials. Day hikes or even a walk in the park can have its share of potential hazards. Encounters with other dogs and animals, broken glass, loose or icy footing, ticks and mosquitoes, dehydration, snakes, almost anything is possible. Day

hikes and car camping as opposed to backpacks most likely will put you nearer to
emergency care and often allow use of your
cellular phone. Even so, the ability to treat
any problem immediately is going to lead to
less severity in any mishap.

So we already have our car restraint and our
pet's identification. Be sure to bring along any
medication your dog takes and bring the same
food and treats he gets at home. I like to pre-
measure each day's meals and pack them in
heavy-duty zip-lock plastic bags and number
them for the days we are going to be gone.
Not only does this insure the food remains dry
and bug-free, but you will know you have the
proper amount for each day and whether or
not you forgot to feed him. Your dog is likely
to be much more active than when at home,
so an increase in food is appropriate. If your
dog is used to sleeping in his crate and you
are car camping, by all means bring it along.
Unless your dog is used to sleeping outside in
cold weather, bring along a coat or doggy
sleeping bag or some way of keeping him
warm. Nights are usually colder than days and
in desert or mountain areas can be radically
lower than daytime temperatures.

Make sure your first-aid kit is complete and

up-to-date. I will cover the items necessary in the chapter on First Aid.

Dog booties, as silly as they may sound, are a critical item to carry on a hike of any distance or for harsh or icy terrain. These just don't seem to stay on very well, so vet wrap which will not rip off all of your dogs fur, will keep them on under almost all conditions. If you can't find vet wrap in the big pet stores, your veterinarian will know where to acquire it.

Dog parkas will keep your dog warm and rain gear is a great item to bring as some dogs take forever to dry. I don't like being wet or cold all day and night and I doubt your dog does either.

Dog sleeping bags or one of your old sleeping bags in cold environments are lifesavers. It may take some coaxing, but your dog will be warm and better off for it. If a sleeping bag is out of the question, a pad or blanket to keep him off the cold ground will keep the chill at bay. My flat-coat retriever just hated sleeping in the tent, so if weather permitted, I tied her down securely near the front of my tent, which has a small roof section, and laid out a blanket or extra clothes for her to lie on. I carried an auger style tie down that screwed into the ground. I can't think of any other way to tie her that she couldn't break away from. Tying your dog to you or your tent would probably get you first prize on America's funniest videos, once she tried to take off! Most parks have rules about keeping your dog inside your tent or RV at night. Be sure and check the rules and laws in your area. Many campgrounds charge extra for dogs and a growing number do not allow dogs at all.

I use a semi-slip collar for my dogs. They are very comfortable when not in use, and tighten just enough to be effective when making corrections without choking or crushing your dog's throat.

A six foot lead is long enough as your dog should really be right next to you at most times. Some trails are just too narrow, so be sure and teach your dog to walk behind you as well as next to you and to not crowd you. Better for you to be the first one to encounter any animal or obstacle.

A long lead or strong rope to tie your dog at the campsite is an option, but those retractable 15-foot leads don't appear to be made terribly strong.

I always carry a carabiner or two, such as rock climber's use, so that I can clip the leash on to my pack or my dogs pack for quick release. If you haven't discovered carabiners yet, check out a store that handles rock-climbing equipment. Ruff Rider carries these as well. I have found at least a dozen good uses for them. Don't trust the cheapies that look the same that you may find at novelty stores or the ones produced as key chains. They are not made to the same standards of rock-climbing equipment.

I feel that a good hiking staff is a necessity on any trip that may involve stream crossings, or hazardous terrain. I like to take mine on most hikes as I never really know what I will encounter and even when maneuvering across any surface that can make my knees or ankles go a different way than my body, it keeps me balanced. My hiking staff also becomes a monopod for steady picture taking at slow shutter speeds or in low light situations.

If you are going on a backpack, a pack for your dog is necessary unless you truly can carry an extra twenty pounds or more. Even so, I'd rather bring twenty pounds worth of food or equipment and train my dog to carry what he needs. A well-conditioned dog can carry up to a third of his weight. I'll go further into detail on this in the pack-training chapter.

Presently there are a wide variety of quality packs being made. I like to use bright
colors for my dog's packs. It helps me to see
them better should they meander off, which
of course shouldn't really happen. Some
packs come with reflective strips sewn in.
Blending into nature is fine, but safety first.
Bright colors may also help prevent some
hunter from thinking your dog is a deer or
bear or whatever animal he is out to hunt. I
call the local ranger station before planning
a trip to find out if hunting is allowed in the
area, and when that season is open.

Collapsible water dishes are easy to find for
dogs and they work well. My dogs were always
taught to be Frisbee dogs, and in the days before
collapsible dishes, the Frisbee also doubled as a
food and water dish.

Today, a quality water purifier is a must. All
backpacking and outdoor type stores carry
them. Both you and your dog are susceptible
to giardia and other bacteria. All streams and
lakes, no matter how far into the wilderness
you go, should be considered tainted. It's a
sad testament to today's environment, but it
is a fact we have to accept. Stopping your
dog from drinking from a stream or lake or
even a puddle may be extremely difficult, but

if you ever have had giardia or know someone who has, you know how important it is
to drink only purified water. Boiling water for
five minutes will kill all the germs, but is
really not a very practical way to get all your
water purified. Plus you are stuck with hot
water unless you have boiled your water
ahead of time and left it out at night to cool.
Iodine tablets in water work also, but are
very hard on you or your dogs system and
should only be used in emergency situations.

I always carry fifteen to twenty feet of high
quality duct tape. There are dozens of uses for
duct tape, as it will hold almost anything together in an emergency. Once I foolishly left my
water filter out overnight and it got well below
freezing. I hadn't emptied it completely and it
froze and cracked. This was the second day of
an eight-day backpack! Duct tape held it together for the duration of the trip. I've used it to
fix broken tent poles, holes in clothes, or build
numerous items.

Next to a water purifier, a well-stocked first-
aid kit is possibly the most important item you
can bring. The chapter on first-aid will detail all
items and their use.

I have a checklist of necessary items for
both my dog and me. The difference between

an overnight trip and a ten-day trip is mostly
the amount of food necessary. The essentials
are still the same. I lay them out all over the
floor and check them off my list as well as
make sure each item is in good working order.
Perishable dates are checked on medical
supplies, water filters, as well as food purchased. Don't forget to load and weigh your
pack and your dog's pack before going on a
backpack. You may have to leave a toy or two
behind.

There was always one item we would forget to bring along before I had a working list.
Having all necessary items as well as all of
our toys makes for a much more enjoyable
trip and after all, this is why we are going!

Chapter

FIRST AID

I t would be impractical to mention every
thing there is to know about first-aid in
this book, but I'd like to go into some detail
about the most common problems and how
to avoid or take care of them immediately.

The woods are lurking with all kinds of
little buggers and critters waiting to scare us
off, but with the right equipment and knowledge, most problems can be avoided or rem-
edied right on the trail. I strongly suggest a
reference guide that will fit in your pack. It
will allow you to grab the information you
need quickly. Knowing what to do is one
thing, but remembering it in a critical situation is often a different story. I still keep a
book in my pack, put out some time ago by
Randy Acker D.V.M. called *A Field Guide / Dog
First Aid / Emergency care for the Hunting,
Working and Outdoor dog.* The American Red
Cross in conjunction with the Humane Society
sells an animal first-aid book that proceeds go
to a good cause. Other books are easily found
on an Internet search.

Your first-aid kit should include all the
items necessary for you and your dog. There
is a page in this book you can copy and use
to check off all the items when you travel.

• For lack of a better place to put this little

tidbit of information, chocolate contains a caffeine-like alkaloid called theobromine. While not toxic to people in the amounts present in commercial foods, these amounts can be quite harmful to dogs. Large amounts can even cause death. If you know your dog has eaten chocolate, induce vomiting. If two or more hours have passed, you would have to administer activated charcoal to prevent the toxin from becoming absorbed.

- Dogs should not be eating your food for many reasons. Besides becoming obnoxious beggars, people food simply isn't good for them no matter how much they like it and how sad they look when they don't get it. There are wonderful recipes to make healthy dog food from certain people foods, but other than that, keep your food out of reach and don't think you are being kind to your dog by giving him people food treats.

First Aid Essentials

The following is my basic first aid kit. It goes in my fanny pack for day hikes or in an easily accessible location in my backpack. Be sure to bring yours up-to-date every year.

Copy this list, or make one for yourself and check off and examine each item at the beginning of every year and especially before any backpack. This first-aid kit is for both you and your dog.

- ❏ Adhesive tape 1" & 2" rolls
- ❏ Gauze bandage rolls 1" & 2"
- ❏ Sterile gauze pads 3" & 4"
- ❏ Medical tape 1" by 10'
- ❏ Scissors
- ❏ Vet wrap
- ❏ Mosquito & Tick repellent
- ❏ Bee sting kit (with an antihistamine and a steroid)
- ❏ Safety pins
- ❏ Neosporin (triple anti-biotic ointment)
- ❏ Boric acid (eye wash)
- ❏ Aspirin
- ❏ Disposable razor
- ❏ Snakebite Kit
- ❏ Tweezers
- ❏ Needle nose pliers (A Leatherman multi-purpose tool has several of the above items)
- ❏ Small squeeze bottle of saline solution (to irrigate and clean a wound)

❏ Small squeeze bottle of Hydrogen
    Peroxide
❏ Diarrhea medicine (tablet form)
❏ Moleskin or Mole foam (for blisters)
❏ Medium butterfly bandages
❏ Regular 1" bandages
❏ Elastic Bandage 4" by 10'
❏ New skin or Second Skin (I prefer the
    swab on and not the spray)
❏ Iodine tablets
❏ Small sewing kit
❏ Ethilon sutures
❏ Alcohol swabs
❏ Quick reference guides for first-aid
    (One for people and one for dogs)

*A pocket comb should be part of your
first aid kit if you are hiking anywhere
where they may be cactus. It works
nicely to push away a stuck piece with
its many spines.

**More is always better than less. If there
are specific medications they can go in
this kit or in a separate container along
with vitamins or any daily pills that you
or your dog need to take. Those daily
pill reminder containers work very well.
The less I have to remember, the more I
can relax!

I strongly suggest you carry at least one of the two books I mentioned on first aid. Everyone should take a course in CPR and basic first-aid if they want to get out into the wilderness. It's good to know wherever you may be.

What needs to be mentioned here that you will not find in a first-aid book, is what to do if something really serious does happen. "Take your dog to the vet" just doesn't work if you are deep into the wilderness on a backpack. It's not likely that you can carry your dog and by doing so in some instances, may further injure him.

Should a serious injury occur, and you cannot get your dog out with you, tie him to a spot that not only provides shelter, but to a place that can easily be found again. You should always know where you are. Mark your map, and be sure and know how to tell a rescuer how to get there. Build a site marker that can be seen from the sky and can be seen from a ground approach as well. If there is a chance that it is going to be cold, put his poncho or your extra jacket on him and leave your blanket or pad for him to lie on. Put some water down if it is appropriate. Clean and cover any open wound. Treat the condition as best as you can and leave a note explaining the situation, should anyone else come along, and then go get help.

If you know you can get him out without further harm and you are not too far off, a litter can be made from a pack frame, tent poles, or sticks, a foam pad and duct tape.

Perhaps I've been lucky. In all my travels we have never had a serious incident. I certainly have heard of them and in almost all cases they could have been prevented. I still believe the wilderness is safer than anywhere in any city and no one should be afraid to take his or her dog with them. Education and preparation will most likely prevent any serious problems from ever occurring.

Chapter

CRITTERS; BIG AND SMALL

Flea and tick powder or spray is a must on any hike. I like Frontline or Advantix. I can't emphasize this enough because ticks are a major vector of illness such as Lyme disease, Ehrlichiosis, RMSF and more. Don't forget, they like dogs just as much as people. A disposable razor for removing hair, tweezers and Neosporin to prevent infection are a must-have in your first aid kit. Check your dog and yourself daily for these critters.

Flea

Ticks

Ticks can carry a slew of diseases, the most common being Lyme disease and Rocky Mountain Spotted fever. There are about 800 kinds of ticks in the world and 100 carry diseases of wildlife, livestock or people. A tick's only food is the blood they suck from their hosts.

Tick

And you thought vampires were a myth! The front part of a tick consists of the head and mouthparts. A tick pushes its hyposteme into a hole in the skin of a host, made from its sharp teeth. Barbs anchor ticks to the skin and make them difficult to pull out. They need to be removed as soon as possible. It may take several days for an infected tick to give a disease to it's host, so the sooner you find it and remove it, the less chance there will be of getting disease.

Ticks must be removed properly in order to be certain that all the mouthparts are removed from the skin. Improper removal may break off the hypostome and become a source of infection or irritation. Also, if you crush them the disease organism may get into the body. People have had many ideas on removing ticks, such as applying clear nail polish or rubbing alcohol, petroleum jelly and using burnt match heads. None of these folklore methods make the tick detach. Ticks must be pulled out. Protected fingers can be used, but blunt curved forceps or tweezers are much easier. Grab the tick as close as possible to where the mouthparts entered the skin, and then steadily pull it out. Take great care not to crush or puncture the body of the tick or get any of its fluids on you. Kill the tick by placing it in alcohol or burn it. Be sure and disinfect the skin with alcohol and wash your hands with soap and water. There is also a device called The Tick Solution that is designed with a spring-loaded pointed forceps.

Mosquitoes

Mosquitoes are everywhere. West Nile virus and other mosquito-borne viruses can cause encephalitis in domestic animals and has killed humans and animals. You or your dog may react with fever, weakness, poor muscle coordination, muscle spasms and signs of a neurological disease, such as change in

Mosquito

temperament or seizures. For yourself, apply insect repellent as indicated on the repellent label. The more DEET a product contains, the longer the repellant can protect against mosquito bites. Contrary to their claims, concentrations higher than 50 percent do not increase the length of protection. For most situations, 10 percent to 25 percent DEET is adequate. Apply repellents to clothes whenever possible; apply sparingly to exposed skin if the label permits. Consult a physician before using repellents on young children.

Advantix also works well in preventing mosquitoes as well as ticks and fleas from biting your dog. It's a once a month topical treatment for dogs and puppies seven weeks and older. The active ingredients are imidacloprid and permethrin.

Snakes

Most snakes are nonpoisonous. There is still a great deal of controversy on how to treat a venomous snakebite. Prevention is of course, the best medicine. There are trainers who give specialized classes in snake avoidance. Dogs seem to be naturally curious of snakes and often times end up getting bit right in the face, so snake avoidance training is money well spent. Dogs are in serious danger once a venomous snake has bitten them. Most dogs are smaller than an adult human therefore there is less mass to absorb the venom. All the old folk remedies are bunk. Keep your dog calm and cease activity, as this will decrease the flow of venom. If the bite is on a leg, put a tourniquet above the bite. It should be tight, but not too tight. Loosen it for thirty seconds every half hour. Use your razor to remove fur, not to cut into the wound, and utilize the suction device in your snakebite kit the same way you would on a person. This needs to be done within sixty seconds and at best it will

only get a bit of the venom out. Snakes don't
always release their venom but there is no
way of knowing other than waiting for symptoms. Baby snakes generally release all of their
venom as opposed to adult snakes that learn to
save their venom for a kill they know they can
eat. Quick and proper treatment may help a bit,
but get your dog to a vet as soon as you can. If
you can carry your dog, do so. It's a good idea
to have done your homework before your trip
and have a piece of paper in the car with the
names and phone numbers of veterinarians in
the general area you are going to be. Most vets
do not have anti-venom as it is extremely
costly and has a short shelf life. Locating a vet
ahead of time that carries anti-venom or at
least has access to getting it may save your
dogs life. Refer to your first aid book on immediate and proper treatment.

Spiders and Scorpions

Spiders and scorpions never were much of
a concern to me until I started bringing my
dog along. I learned early in my camping
days to never blindly reach into anything and
to keep in the back of my mind that there can
be spiders anywhere and when in scorpion
country, to be a bit more cautious. Black

widow spiders and scorpions are nocturnal, but that doesn't mean that they can't be active during the day when you expose them from their hiding places.

Dogs have no wisdom when it comes to these critters and it is up to you to be your dogs' brain when these critters are around. There is no reason to be afraid all the time and let any of natures little nuisances prevent you from enjoying your trip. Just keep it in the back of your mind, and if your dog should act sick or much different than normal, try to find the cause. It is impossible to find spider bite marks on a longhaired dog, but on the other hand, many dogs have thick coats that prevent a lot of critters from getting through. Spider bites, as opposed to insect bites and bee stings, the swelling can last for days or even weeks. There may be sloughing of the tissue at the site of the bite and in some instances can lead to death. Unless there is an allergic reaction to bee stings, no treatment is necessary.

Toads

Toads all have a bad taste, but dogs don't know that until they mouth them. In the south, tropical toads (Bufo marinus) can be a serious concern. They secrete a toxin that appears to affect the heart and circulation of dogs and can lead to death as quickly as fifteen minutes. Symptoms depend on the toad and the amount of toxin absorbed. Signs vary from slobbering to convulsion and death. If you know that your dog has mouthed a toad, flush his mouth out with a hose should you be in a camping area that has one, or induce vomiting and be prepared to give your dog artificial respiration.

Porcupines

The important thing to remember about removing a porcupine quill is to remove the whole thing. Grasp the quill with your pliers near the point where it disappears into the skin, then with a quick tug, pull it out. Do not ignore pieces that you cannot pull out. They can work their way down into bone or internal organs, carrying infection with them. If you broke off a piece and cannot remove it, you will need to take your dog to the vet.

Alligators

Alligators are only in a few states in the US, but many dogs lose their lives to them. Slow as they may appear, they can move quite quickly when least expected. Though I have not hiked in alligator country, from talking to a few people who have, and a few people who have lost their pets to these pre-historic creatures, the vast majority of incidences would have been avoided had their dog been on a leash.

Bears

I like to avoid bear country when I camp with my dogs. It is possible for a dog to provoke a bear, but if your dog is on leash, this should not occur. I don't feel that Black bears are a threat to humans unless we do something very stupid. Black bears are one of the most intelligent mammals. I just don't want to have to think about them and I especially do not like the task of bear bagging my food and my dog's food every day. Many parks today require you carry your food in small bear-proof containers. They can be purchased or rented for as little as a dollar a day. Extra weight if you are a backpacker!

Some Black bears go by different names like Kermode bear, Cinnamon bear, or Glacier bear, but they are all Black bears. Grizzly's are quite different and do pose a true threat. There are approximately one thousand Grizzly bears in the lower forty-eight states. I've yet to see one anywhere but in Canada, but it's a good idea to find out if they roam the area you will be hik-

ing. They can be found in Wyoming, Montana
and Idaho.

   If you are hiking or camping in Black bear
territory without a bear-proof container, I
hope that everyone knows or learns how to
properly bear-bag their food. Bears are capable of learning every technique possible to
get food. Putting your food in a stuff sack and
over a very tall branch is what everyone
knows, but tying it off to the trunk of the tree
is an easy task for most bears to figure out.
They will either pull or tear that rope and all
of your food is gone. Use another stuff sack
and either divide up the food in equal weight
between bags, or put anything in it to equal
the weight of your food bags. This needs to
be tossed up around a branch high enough so
that only you and a long stick can reach the
stuff sacks. Bears can get up mighty high on
two legs with arms stretched. Black bears can
also climb trees very easily, so your food has
to be far enough out on a branch that is too
thin or weak for a bear to venture that far out.
Be sure to keep food out of your tent. That is a
dangerous way to attract an unwanted visitor!

   Bears are the only animal worth going into
any detail about, mostly because they are so
darn smart and because they have little to no

**Improper
Bear-bagging**

**Proper
Bear-bagging**

fear of humans or a single dog. Mountain lions, porcupines, badgers, wolverines, moose, wolves, deer, elk, raccoons, coyotes and just about any animal out there has the ability to kill or cause great harm to your dog, but they all fear adult humans and as long as your dog is in your control, they should pose no threat. Dogs that are left alone are easy prey for any of these animals. Never leave your dog unattended. If your trip involves you doing things on your own, best not to take your dog along unless someone else will be able to watch them. Use your carabiner to clip your dogs' lead to your belt or pants if you need to use two hands to carry firewood or water. If "nature calls" and you are walking off to do what you have to do, bring your dog and tie her to you or a rock or tree until you are finished. There really is no reason why your dog should be unattended or out of sight at any time.

I remember the first time I had attended a seminar about wilderness first-aid. I became so aware of all the things that "can happen" I started thinking that staying home was a better idea. Then it occurred to me that I had spent literally thousands of hours hiking, camping and other outdoor activities without mishap.

It's no different than knowing not to stand under that lone tree in a thunderstorm. At first, the knowledge of "what can happen" is overwhelming. Once put into proper perspective, knowing what to do when something happens, or better yet, how to prevent these things from happening; there is no reason to be fearful of the outdoors. People are far more unpredictable than insects or wild animals. We are just more used to being in an urban environment.

Even from a percentage standpoint, the likeliness of being hurt while driving your car is far greater than being injured while out in the woods or deserts.

I'll take my chances with nature any day. In all the years I've been hiking and backpacking, the only times I've ever had any injuries were from falling, and those were few. Other than being sore and embarrassed, I never needed any medical attention beyond cold water, a band-aid and anti-biotic cream.

Stuff happens, and it's good to be aware of it, but let good judgment be your guide. Not fear.

Chapter 6

BASIC TRAINING

J ust like a child, patience and praise go a
long way when training dogs. Most dogs
are capable of learning far more than we
every try teaching them. In future chapters I
will discuss pack training and trail readiness.

It is essential that your dog has mastered
the basics of obedience training in order to
move on to pack training. Every dog needs
to be a well-trained, obedient dog. Not
only does this make life better for the
owner, but when dogs know they are doing the things that please their owners,
they become better and happier pets.

Once we start taking our dogs outdoors,
without a strong command of the basics in
training, we will not only have a difficult time
teaching proper trail manners, but their safety
is at risk. Most dogs do not generalize very well
so be sure your dog knows his commands
outdoors as well as indoors.

Along with the standard, sit, down, stay, heel
etc– teaching your dog to come when called,
no matter what activity he is involved in, is
paramount.

I am a strong advocate of teaching hand
signals used in conjunction with basic verbal
commands. Often, hand signals prove to be
more effective than their verbal counterparts,

since there can be many situations where the background noise is very loud, or you simply do not want to break the silence and disturb the wildlife.

It is estimated that thirty percent of Dalmatians are born deaf. These dogs learn hand commands without any verbal prompt. Most dogs are very aware visually and hand signals used in conjunction with spoken commands will aid your dog in understanding what is required of them.

I've read of a deaf Dalmatian that learned numerous hand signs in American Sign Language, (ASL) which is far more complicated than basic hand signals for dogs. There are dogs specifically trained to aid people with severe hearing loss. These dogs are generally retrievers and labs as they are most acute in sight and are more easily trained than some other breeds.

I'd also like to point out that verbal commands need not be shouted. Best that they are not. Some dogs come to think that the only time you are serious is when you shout. Any voice, even a whisper will do, as long as it is heard.

Contrarily, developing a good loud whistle is very useful in getting your dog to return to you should he wander off or be in a noisy environment. Always be sure to praise him for coming to you rather than yelling for wandering off. Of course had he been leashed, this never would have occurred.

It's very important to incorporate different environments in your training. Just because you are training your dog for the trail, does not mean you won't have to cross some roads, or get out of the car near busy highways. Getting your dog used to traffic and other possible aversions will help avoid any possibility of panic or surprise at a potentially dangerous time. The more situations your dog is exposed to, the less likely the unexpected will scare him.

Allow your dog to get used to other people as well as animals such as horses, cattle, cats and especially other dogs. These animals and others are likely to be encountered on trails, therefore early exposure will help keep your dog calm and focused when you are hiking or camping. The earlier in a dogs life you can socialize him, the easier it will be. It is estimated that ninety percent of a dogs socialization skills are developed from three to five months old.

Train your dog on a variety of different terrains, such as grass, dirt, rocks, hills and near streams. Dogs need to learn how to swim. Throwing him in can be traumatic and not all dogs figure out what to do in an instant. That type of training is archaic and is just as bad as doing it to young children. Perhaps even worse, since you can discuss children's trauma with them, but a dog may just have a fear that lasts their lifetime.

It's fine to begin trail training as young as three or four months, but a puppy's muscular and skeletal systems are still very immature. Start with a towel lying across his back where a pack would go. We will go into further detail about pack training in the chapters that follow.

Early focus should be on behavior. Do not try to build stamina in a young dog. Please remember that this needs to be fun for your dog, not boot camp. Keep work times down to ten or fifteen minutes to begin. Let them play a little bit and go around smelling everything in their new environment. It is their way of processing information, as they will develop their sense of smell in all of these new places so that they may identify what is natural to the area.

I've found that most any dog at any age can learn to be a more disciplined and knowledgeable trail dog if this basic formula is applied.

Even if your goal is simply to go for a stroll in the neighborhood or park, a trained dog that understands what is expected of him can turn a potential frustrating or dangerous walk into a pleasurable one.

Clicker training has been the rage in training young and old dogs. It is both a technology and training philosophy. Karen Pryor popularized the term and the practice of clicker training. In her book, *Don't Shoot The Dog* from 1985, she captured the public's interest, which led to a widespread assumption that this was something new. Karen explains in her introduction that clicker training is based on the science and technology of operant conditioning and has been used since the 1940's. I have seen the results of clicker training and they are amazing.

I have always been an advocate of positive training, and I have successfully trained my dogs by positive methods. I believe in making corrections and using the word "no" along with a great deal of praise when my dogs do what I am trying to teach them.

I also see no problem in the use of treats when training. Many people are under the assumption they will always have to use treats to get their dogs to do what they command.

Weaning them off constant treats is not a problem. Your happiness and praise are important and their conditioning to your commands will be engrained.

Since this is not a book on basic dog training, as there are numerous books on the subject, I can only tell you to read as many books as you can get your hands on. You will find many different philosophies and methods of training. I would say most trainers today use clickers. Their effectiveness cannot be denied. As clicker training is completely positive training, you will always see a happy dog with his tail going ninety miles an hour. Dogs that are punished and screamed at will learn also, but teaching with fear does not produce a happy dog or a dog that looks forward to further training.

Melissa C. Alexander's book *Click For Joy* is wonderfully informative and won a Maxwell award for best book on training and behavior. Karen Pryor's *Clicker Training* is also a fantastic book. There of course, are countless others that offer sound advice and philosophies. My suggestion is to read as many as you can and see what feels right and works for you and your dog. The Monks of New Skeete have some of the most wonderful

books on understanding and training dogs
using non-clicker methods.

I do feel that it is important that these
early outings be a one-on-one relationship.
A second person or dog often interrupts the
rapport. Outings with other hikers and their
dogs can be a lot of fun, and is great for
socialization, but it is the wrong setting for
early training purposes.

A veteran hiking dog can adapt to most
changes and distractions, but random play of
other dogs and the chatter of other people
will distract a novice dog.

Once basic obedience training skills have
been well engrained, it's time to move on to
pack training. Even if your dog will never
wear a pack and you don't intend on going
on long backpacks, the chapters that follow
may still be obstacles you encounter.

Please don't expect your dog to overcome
all obstacles at first. Each trip is a valuable
lesson and life is constant learning experience.

Chapter 7

PACK TRAINING

It's fine to begin pack training as young as three or four months, but a puppy's muscular and skeletal systems are quite immature. You can get your puppy acquainted with carrying a pack by simply placing a proper size towel across his back and secure it with a piece or two of ribbon or soft material. It won't be long until he associates that having a towel (eventually a pack) across his back means hiking and fun. Once he gets to be the size he will be as an adult, you can start using the pack. At first keep it empty and continue your routine of pack equals hiking which equals fun. Bones and cartilage are not mature until about twelve to fifteen months in most breeds and some breeds such as Rottweilers, Shepards, and Belgians are not mature until they are two and a half years old. Consult your vet for information on your dogs' breed.

Pack training is no more than teaching your dog how to walk with you and how to behave while wearing his pack. Most dogs are taught to walk to the immediate left of you and to not pull or get ahead of you. They need to walk your pace and not be walking with their head to the ground looking and sniffing every little thing. You are in charge, not your dog. When you stop, he needs to stop and sit. Sitting will keep him from being face down checking out everything on the ground. Instead he will be looking at you and waiting for his next command. As you step forward, he starts out with you and again keeps pace. If you leave your dog in charge of the pace and how and where to walk, you will never get far and you will end up a slave to your dogs whims. Playtime is later. Now is time for putting on a little distance and actually getting somewhere in a harmonious and peaceful fashion.

Fit the pack to your dog at home or somewhere where there are no distractions. Teaching him to stand on command is something most people never consider. It's quite helpful in this instance. I feel it is better to start your adjustments at your dogs head as he will be more comfortable seeing you and having you praise him from there. That is certainly not carved in stone. You will soon find out what works best with you and your dog.

The packs I have used and recommend are Wenaha packs, which was the first pack I ever purchased. They do not directly sell their packs. I purchased mine at an REI store. They now have the Explorer II which I have not tested. It's two-piece, meaning that you strap on the basic harness and then the packs lie

across it and stay on with the Velcro sewn into
both pieces. It stood up to every test I gave it
and to this day I can't say if the advantage of
being able to take the pack part off separately
for resting or adjustment is a better system
then a one-piece pack. The one-piece packs I
have used are Jandd Mountaineering's Kelev
pack www.jandd.com and The Banzai pack
made by Wolf Packs, www.wolfpacks.com
Both are absolutely top notch.

Jandd Mountaineering out of California is
much better known for bicycle accessories,
but they put out one heck of a pack for dogs
and have been for well over a decade. Wolf
Packs is a small company out of Oregon that
hand makes their fantastic line of dog packs
and accessories and have also been around
for more than a decade. Not only are all of
these packs well made, but the companies
that make them are wonderful to deal with
and all very ecologically involved.

Whether you are using a one-piece or two-
piece pack, proper size and placement are
very important. The pack should ride over the
shoulders, not way down on the back. (see
illustration) Make sure the pack does not
impede your dog's movement. You don't
want the straps chafing your dog's chest or

Proper Pack Placement

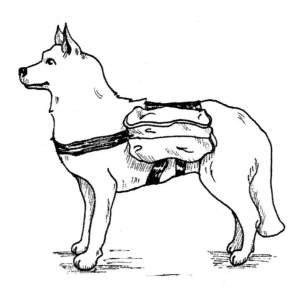

Improper Pack Placement

stomach. Weight over the kidneys is just as uncomfortable to them as it is to you. The panniers should hang to about the bottom of your dog's chest, while making sure that the yoke is wide enough for your dogs back.

Once your dog is comfortable walking with his pack on, he is ready for a little bit more. Fill it with towels or something soft and light and stuff it so it is approximately the size it would be when almost full. Make sure both sides are even. He needs to learn he is much wider than he was before!

Early focus should be on behavior. Do not try to build stamina with a young dog. Keep your work times short and let your dog play a little bit and go around sniffing and smelling everything in his new environment once you have stopped for a rest.

If you are training an adult dog that has never worn a pack, use the same formula as above, starting with the empty pack. He still needs to get used to carrying a pack and needs positive re-enforcement to understand this is going to be fun!

Most packs have a D-ring to attach the leash. I feel that attaching the leash to his semi-slip collar is better as pulling on the pack may cause it to slip or tilt from side to side. Having the leash on his collar will also give you control when you take his pack off.

Once you start loading actual items, equal weight, bulk and balance are imperative. Keep softer items toward the dog, and heavier items at the bottom. If there is an item that you will be taking out of the pack often, keep it near the top so you don't have to disturb your nicely balanced packing.

Build up to the desired weight load gradually. Assuming you have a sixty-pound adult dog, and you've got him used to the pack and the wide load, start with about seven pounds and hike with that weight for a while. Increase gradually over time to the weight you feel he will be able to carry based on his breed and experience. A twenty-pound load on a sixty-pound dog is the limit and that is based on a well-trained dog suited for that kind of burden. That's a third of his weight! For most dogs, I do not recommend going over 25% of their weight. This formula will also tell you how many days you can be on a backpack with your dog, unless you are willing to carry some of his food or supplies. My dogs were able to eventually carry 33% of their weight. Trips were planned accordingly. I carried all my stuff,

and they carried all of theirs. It seemed fair
to me!

I've known some people who planned a
three-day backpack and figured that since
their dog was only carrying three days worth
of food, she could carry some of their toys.
Boy was he unhappy when he discovered
how banged up those items were inside the
dogs pack. Get a mule or a llama if you want
a beast of burden!

Teach your dog to walk behind you without
crowding you, as well as the standard position
of walking immediately to your left side. Trails
are often only wide enough for one person,
and the middle of the wilderness is not the
place to teach your dog anything new. I have
him sit on my left as if we were going to walk
in a normal fashion and then give him a command to stay. Take a step in front of him and
then start out and give him a command to
come, but make sure he stays behind you. You
can make up any word you want here, as long
as it doesn't sound too much like other commands. Back, or behind, will work. This is
much easier to do if you can practice on a trail
that is only wide enough for one. Your dog
will be confused at first until he eventually
discovers that you do in fact want him behind

you. Control him with his leash and tell him he's a good boy or however you assure your dog he is doing the correct thing. Stay in front of him and keep him behind you while using the command you chose as well as rewards or assurance. There will be a lot of crashing into you as well as him trying to get over on your left, where he thinks he belongs. In time he will understand. It becomes much more obvious when the trail only allows single file, but that situation can not be easily recreated, so mix up the training of walking behind you as well as to your side. Eventually he will understand what is expected of him and once put to use in a real situation, a little light bulb may click and it will make more sense. Dogs don't really need to know why, as much as how and what is expected of them. Their rational is generally much different than ours!

First outings with a full pack should be approximately thirty-minute hikes. Find a nice loop to hike or time your hike in so you don't end up going too far before turning around and going back. If you can simulate all of the different terrain you will eventually be hiking, all the better!

Everything your dog does with his pack on is a new experience. He will eventually find your pace and soon there will be no more stepping on heels, or crashing into you. Attention should be mutual here. The hiker must learn to listen to his dogs breathing and footsteps. If your dog stops, so should you, whatever the reason. Often, it is just to relieve himself. Perhaps he has picked up a smell that has aroused his attention. Maybe something is stuck in his paw. I believe that it is important that your dog knows that you respect his needs and curiosity. This is the making of a partnership. After all, he is along to share in your experiences.

Chapter

TRAIL ETIQUETTE 101

I t's very important to teach your dog the proper action and reaction when encountering other hikers on the trail. Keep him right behind you or immediately to your side, and either keep hiking if the trail is wide, or have him come to the heel position. He will most likely feel secure by your side. If other hikers show interest in your dog, give him the OK or whatever release command you use and allow the hikers to approach. If he starts to get defensive or protective keep him close and again reassure him with "it's ok" or whatever he is used to. Never let him run up to other hikers. Even if you know he's never bitten anyone in his entire life, they don't know it. I know I'm not comfortable having some strange dog running at me!

Approaching other dogs seems to be the most difficult encounter on the trail. Many aren't leashed or under control. In these instances I let my dog go ahead of me a bit. Not only is it natural to dogs, but if he is forced to stay behind, it signals weakness to the other dog. Keep him leashed, keep voices friendly and see if it is appropriate to let the dogs check each other out, or if you need to keep him at your side.

Dogfights are uncommon in the outdoors but are always a possibility. There is common territory, but there are owners to protect. Some dogs will fight for dominance also. I don't allow any of it. Not with strange dogs, strange people and strange settings.

If both dogs are leashed, there will be no problems. If the approaching dog is looking for a fight and the owner is foolish enough to allow it or doesn't know what to do, one procedure is to determine which dog is losing and pull his back legs out from him. Even if it is your dog! This is not an easy thing to do and it must be done with a great deal of assertiveness or you will only cause the losing dog to slip and panic, which will increase his chance of being bitten. You stand a good chance of being bitten as well. I know I'll get a lot of arguments on this theory, but I've yet to have anyone give me better advice unless they carry pepper spray. Carrying pepper spray would be the safest way to break up the dogs, but it is painful and a last resort. I don't bring it on backpacks, but I recommend it on all other hikes or in public camping areas. Just don't be too quick to use it, as most fights are all talk and little action. The majority of times when two dogs meet on neutral ground, they simply go through their sniffing and identifying rituals, perhaps a show of dominance and that's it.

When we hike we share the trail with many others. When meeting up with horses or a team of mules or llamas, you and your dog should always give up the right of way. Pull yourselves as far off the trail as you can, tell your dog it's ok, and wait until they have passed.

Encounters with wild animals are rare but not do occur. It's important to remember that this is their home and they were not out looking for you or your dog. Every day is life and death survival to them. Having your dog chase them off could make the difference of the animal's survival.

Some animals are just mean by nature, such as moose, badgers wolverines and alligators to name a few. Porcupines know you can't take them on and skunks know what to do when they are cornered. Survival is an every day affair to wild animals and even the smallest and cutest ones can be tremendously vicious when cornered.

I'm convinced that having your dog on lead and under control and having a little bit of smarts about where you are hiking and what you may encounter, will give 99% assurance of a safe trip.

The Canine Hikers Bible from Cruden Bay Books, is an excellent resource of where we can and cannot bring our dogs as well as rules and regulations for the areas shown. Regulations and restrictions change often, so be sure and check on the area you intend on hiking, before you go.

The next chapter falls under the heading of trail etiquette as well, but since so many people got such a kick out of it in previous books, I'll keep it as a chapter unto itself.

Chapter

DOES A DOG POOP IN THE WOODS?

O f course he does!
I realize this is not the type of subject people want to discuss in great detail, but its importance cannot be denied. It is one of many reasons why trails and campgrounds are being closed off to dogs.

Parks and campgrounds have specific rules about picking up after your dog. If you are in doubt as what to do when there are no hard and fast rules, just put yourself in the place of the next person who uses that campsite or comes down the trail your dog just pooped on. Is this what you want to see, or worse, step in?

Essentially, animals will be animals. Just because wolves, rabbits and yes, even bears defecate in the woods wherever and whenever, does not give you the same privilege. You are in their house, remember?

A good argument is that horses leave their tremendous messes on the trail and no one is stopping and picking that up.

Hard to argue with that, but it is quite ridiculous to expect someone to be picking up after a team of horses and it is widely accepted that no one does. I've had my fill of stepping around horse crap for miles and miles. I finally stopped taking most of the trails that were used by horses. The flies that follow are reason enough to go a different route.

The fact still remains, that I will not leave anything on the trail, or near a campground, that I wouldn't want to see myself. If my dog has to poop on the trail, it just isn't that difficult to bury it, or toss it off where no one else has to deal with it.

Around the campsite, not only do I not want to smell it, but I don't relish the possibility of stepping in it! And don't forget about the flies it attracts.

The proper procedure is the same as you should be using for yourself. Bury it six inches below the ground. It is easy, a safe depth to walk on, and the correct depth for quick decomposition.

Picking it up and packing it out on a walk in the neighborhood, or a park or public camping area is best, but on an honest-to-goodness backpack, burying it is the only choice for me.

The next time you set up camp and it is clean and free from any evidence that anyone else was ever there, I hope you appreciate it and leave it the same way.

Enough said about this. Let us move on.

Chapter

ADVERSE WEATHER AND HAZARDOUS TERRAIN

No matter where you hike, there is always the possibility of adverse weather. Seems to me that the weather forecasters don't do much better than the flip of a coin, so be prepared for the worst-case scenario depending on the area and time of the year. At least half the horror stories I have heard involved hikers and campers that were unprepared for an adverse change in weather.

Temperatures in desert areas drop radically in the night and high mountain regions are completely unpredictable. Every part of the country has radical weather conditions and we can be prepared for most of them.

I remember a backpack I was on in August at about 11,000 ft. on the east side of the Sierra mountain range. I was down by the lake nearby wearing only my shorts. It was a gorgeous day, probably 70 degrees with sunshine and a clear sky. It seemed that in the blink of an eye, the temperature dropped and ice balls started falling from the sky! Ouch! My buddy's tent was about one hundred and fifty yards away. I ran as fast as I could (barefoot) and dove in his tent. He had been only a few feet from his tent stringing his fly rod, so he was already inside and saw that I was on my way. The temperature must have dropped thirty or forty degrees and for at least 20 minutes, it was dark and hail kept falling from the sky. My tent was another hundred yards, but I wasn't going anywhere. I put on his jacket, sweats and socks and we watched and waited it out.

Had we been on a day hike, with only shorts and a t-shirt, miles from our camp, we may have found shelter from a boulder, as we were above tree limit, but it would have been painful while looking and shivering cold crouching there waiting out the freezing weather. Ever since that episode, I've always brought my fanny pack with a first aid kit, stocking cap, mosquito net, flashlight with spare batteries and bulb, iodine, water bottle, emergency kit with lighters, matches, candles, space blanket and rope, rubber tips for my constantly freezing feet, and some type of rain jacket.

That is just one instance of strange and unexpected weather. There have been many more.

Snow and Cold

Dogs, just like us, need to become acclimated to their environment. When a dog has not been gradually accustomed to snow and cold, the weather will be a shock to his system. Dogs can get used to extreme cold temperatures if they are slowly introduced. Problem is, most of the time we don't have the time or proper conditions to prepare. This is where extra clothes, cover, booties and sleeping bags for dogs can be a huge plus. Most of the newer tents have a vestibule that offers decent protection without having your dog walk all over your sleeping bag or tearing holes in the bottom of your tent. Which reminds me to point out to clip your dogs nails a week or two before you hike so they will be the proper length and not tender. If you do keep your dogs in the tent with you, an extra tarp will help stop the floor from being torn.

I'm a firm believer in hiking with a hiking staff. There are now many to choose from. Some people still like the nostalgic five or six foot gnarly stick, but back in my early fly-fishing days, I had started using a metal pole that had a comfortable rubber handle and an interchangeable tip, from rubber to a sharp metal point. Currents were fast, rocks were slick and three legs is the best balance on any terrain. Hence the use of tripods!

When hiking in snowy areas, the hiking staff not only aids your balance, but also works as a probe to check the snow or ice to see if there is safe footing.

Remember to make frequent stops when hiking with your dog over snowy areas, as ice balls form between the pads of your dog's feet. If left unattended, they can cut deeply and injure your dog. Paws that are constantly wet can develop bacterial or fungal infections. Road salt, or most chemicals used to melt ice can be very irritating. If the salt or chemicals are licked, it can even cause internal damage. Check occasionally for faint blood marks in paw prints. Even though the paws may look perfectly normal, the cold weather brings the warming blood to the surface of the paw. This is a warning that your dog has extended his system in order to maintain. Resting usually helps and symptoms generally subside. If the pattern repeats, then all activity should be halted.

Dog booties may sound silly, but they can aid in the prevention of all of these problems. If the booties on your dog seem to come off too easily, vet wrap will secure them and not rip all of your dogs fur when removing them.

There are products on the market made to protect pads. I have no personal experience with them, nor have I spoken to anyone who has used them. Perhaps we will be able to review them on our web site some day. The old method is to use petroleum jelly or baby oil on pads to protect them.

Same as people, dogs have no traction on ice and trouble with footing in deep snow. Be sure and pay very close attention for glazed slopes, or any possible area that loss of traction would result in an accident. If absolutely necessary, unclip the lead line so that your dog can navigate through the trees. If there is a particularly hazardous or slippery area, it may be best to wrap the lead around your hand several times so you can keep your dog close by. Snow and cold will inhibit your dog's ability to find his way by sense of smell, so a bright pack and a close eye are very important.

Skijoring, which is cross-country skiing with dogs, is a wonderful sport and a topic that would be far too lengthy for a book of this nature. It's gaining in popularity, but many cross country skiers are not familiar with this activity. Demonstrating thoughtfulness and picking up after your dog will help with the image this sport portrays.

I've never participated, but it looks like a great deal of fun. They have their own language when it comes to commands for the dogs. Go is "hike" turn right is "gee" left is "haw" and the command to slow down is "easy". I guess they couldn't think of something new for that one!

Snow shoeing is nicely paced, and allows for a quiet winter hike. Problem is, our little four-footed friends leave a mighty narrow print and can easily fall through deep snow.

Heat and Dehydration

Hiking in warm weather can be dangerous for your dog unless you are careful to monitor him and allow your dog to drink all he wants. Your dog is at a disadvantage because he can only sweat from his tongue and paw pads.

There are several ways to check for dehydration. Lift up his skin above the shoulder blades and let go. It should drop right back in place if your dog is properly hydrated. Watch for signs of heat distress, such as rapid pulse, constant panting, red gums or if

his ears, nose or throat feel dry and hot. More serious symptoms are vomiting, glassy eyes, diarrhea and weakness.

Should you discover that dehydration has gone into those stages, of course taking him to the vet is always the textbook answer, but whether or not that is possible, do everything you can to cool him down. Wrap wet clothing around him and give him drops of water. Submerging into a cold stream is too much of a shock to his system.

Another byproduct of a hot day is hot surfaces. Dirt trails don't generally get too hot, but pavement can be burning hot to your dog's pads. If the pavement feels hot to your hands, it's hot to your dog's feet as well.

Most people don't realize that dogs can also be prone to sunburn. Light-skinned dogs are especially susceptible. A good thick coat of fur will protect from cold as well as heat. Noses, especially light colored ones, are susceptible to sunburn. You can use sun block on your dogs nose, just be sure it is non-toxic, as they will most likely lick it.

I'd like to mention once again the dangers of drinking non-purified water. All streams, lakes, ponds, and puddles are considered tainted water. Your dog is just as susceptible to all the water born protozoa as you are. The main culprit is Giardia Lamblia. It lives and grows in your dog's intestines as easily as yours. People often tell me that their dog has been drinking out of streams for years and have never had a problem. I'm very glad for them. I'd rather prevent the possibility than hope that I'm lucky every time. This just isn't the same earth it was only a couple of decades ago. Dogs stand even a better chance of getting giardia because if they swim or walk through the water and lick their fur, it can be transmitted that way!

Symptoms generally appear one to two weeks after ingestion. The most common sign is diarrhea. It can be severe and even bloody. If it goes untreated, it can continue indefinitely. The good news is it is generally cured with antibiotics with about 90% effectiveness.

If I could remove any two living organisms from this earth they would be mosquitoes and giardia protozoa's.

Another nasty thing that lives in untreated water is algae. There are different types of

algae in differerent parts of the country.
Listing them all may be interesting, but to
sum it up, algae can actually be deadly. All
the more reason not to take any chances
and treat all water as poison, unless properly treated.

Hazardous Terrain

Nature never fails to throw its share of hazardous terrain at us on just about any trip
short of a walk in the park or around the
neighborhood. If it isn't the weather, it will
surely be obstacles such as stream crossings,
narrow trails, drop-offs and rock or boulder
scrambling.

If it is at all possible to practice some of
these situations on a local day hike, take full
advantage of it rather than finding out how
you will fare on a trip far from any help.

Map out your trip and try and figure out just
what type of terrain you may encounter.
Stream crossing in spring can be nearly impossible whitewater when that same trip in
fall will just be a gentle creek.

I like to map out alternate hikes in case the
obstacles we encounter are just too much of
a danger. At least my trip won't be over and
often times I've ended up exploring a beauti-

ful place I may have never considered. There is one such place that I have been back to at least once a year over the course of eleven years.

Stream Crossings

f you and your dog have crossed a few simple creeks and streams he will have more confidence to attempt a larger one. Unless you are crossing one or two feet of slow moving water with a soft pebble bottom, stream crossings can be very dangerous.

Your dog's pack should be removed before attempting a difficult stream. It is extra weight and even heavier if it gets wet. Some packs have drain holes that aid in drying, but they won't move water if the pack is submerged.

Try and cross streams at their widest point. The water level will always be lowest there. Be sure there is no steep bank on the other side. If the water level is up to your dogs pack, tie him off and set his pack down and cross the stream yourself. If you are wearing gators, remove them first. I always carry a hiking staff and this is where it becomes most valuable. More often than not, streams have very slippery rock bottoms. I also use my staff to check for holes in the riverbed or root tangles. Be sure to keep your feet at shoulder width or as they say, keep your feet under you. Unclip the waist belt of your pack for quick removal if necessary. I like to loosen the laces of my boots in case they should get stuck I can still get my foot out. You may want to change into shorts and your spare shoes to keep your boots and pants dry.

Face slightly upstream for stability and also to see what is floating your way.

Once you have negotiated your way across, remove your pack and head back as close to the same route as possible.

Though it was most likely torture for your dog to watch you cross a river without him, he will have seen your successful trek and perhaps have a bit more confidence when it's the two of you.

If necessary, grab his pack and make the trip one more time alone. This will all depend on the severity of the stream crossing.

Don't even think about carrying him across. This is a definite formula for disaster!

Now your packs are on the other side, and you are ready to cross the stream with your dog. I like to use my caribiner and clip my dogs lead to my belt. This gives me both hands and no chance of losing the lead. You can still keep the lead in one hand while your staff is in the other. Walk in slowly, don't drag him in. You should be acting and speaking calmly. You've made this trek twice already, four times if you count both ways. If there was any doubt in your mind about the safety of this crossing, it's time to get out the map and see where there may be a wider crossing or slower moving current. You may need to find a different destination.

Move through the water slowly and steadily. When you've reached the other side, tell your hiking buddy what a good dog he has been. With all that water around that he wasn't allowed to drink, this is a good time to give him some purified water so that he is less apt to try a drink from the stream or to get moisture from liking his fur.

Dry yourselves off and you are ready for more adventure!

Bouldering

Almost anywhere you hike in the United States you may encounter boulders. Random House unabridged dictionary defines a boulder as "a detached and rounded or worn rock, esp. a large one." Of course now we need to define "large". I would say bigger than you could throw, all the way up to big enough to climb. In any case, there are boulders every-where. Even in the desert.

Boulders in canyons or rivers are generally very smooth and quite slick when they get wet. Other boulders such as granite are as tough as heavy sandpaper. Imagine walking on either of these in your bare feet! I almost never go barefoot so I'm a total tenderfoot. Some people can navigate boulders and some are tough enough to walk on granite all day, but they didn't start out that way. Most dogs see carpet, linoleum, tile and grass for better than 95% of the day. Perhaps some pound the smooth pavement for a mile or two.

You've got your expensive hiking boots and your dog is essentially barefoot. Hopefully you brought booties in case pads do get tender. I understand that tannic acid made from tea applied to dogs pads before a hike, can toughen them up a bit. There are several over-the-counter products that make this claim as well. It's hard to tell if it actually works, but it probably couldn't hurt. Better yet, gradually work your dog up to handling rough granite, or a balance job on a slick rock. The more prepared he is, the less chance of any problems once you finally get out for that long deserved camping trip or backpack.

Most dogs jump from boulder to boulder with no problem. After a bit of experience dogs are a good judge of their leaping ability. You will have to be the judge if a trail starts looking too difficult. We have hands to climb and less horizontal mass to move from rock to rock.

If your dog is wearing a pack, it needs to be snug and perfectly balanced. Be sure and check often to see that the pack is still straight. The pack gets knocked around a lot. I also remove the lead for this type of travel.

It's quite common that dogs' pads can be lacerated from traversing boulder fields or scree slopes. Even dogs with tough pads can get cut or worn, especially from granite. Be sure and check pads on a timely basis and if you see them worn or cut, stop immediately. If they are bleeding, direct pressure with a clean dressing will stop it. Check all pads and put booties on your dog. I don't wait to see if the booties will stay up, I put the vet wrap over them right away.

This will be awkward and unnatural to your dog and he will also have much less traction. This is the time to evaluate whether or not you should go on, turn back, or stay where you are for a while. These types of injuries do not heal quickly. If your dog is wearing a pack, it would be best if you carried it.

Stop often and check for swelling. If there is swelling, loosen the vet wrap and move as slowly and easily as you can. You should either stay put for a while or head back to the car if the injury is not too bad. The trip should be over just as it would be if you injured your foot. Dogs just don't complain like people do.

Cliffs and Drop-Offs

Cliffs and steep drop-offs freak out most people and dogs as well. Navigating them is 50% balance and 50% confidence.

These situations are always dangerous and if you add loose soil or stones it gets really freaky.

I believe the lead line should be removed. Your dog's pack should be perfectly balanced and if the situation is a drop-off next to a slope or boulders, the pack should be removed. Even after the many miles my dogs have carried their packs, they still were a poor judge of how much wider they were with their packs on.

Most dogs have much better balance than we do and though the cliffs may frighten them, it's a natural instinct of potential danger and not a re-occurring image of them falling down the cliff.

I do my very best to avoid these situations, but they usually are unexpected. If it really looks dangerous I just go back. It's never worth the risk. Better to live and hike another day!

Chapter

LONG TRIPS

Once you have established your campsite and packs are removed, I like to investigate my immediate surroundings with my dog. Once his pack is off, or the car gets unloaded, he is apt to break some of the rules he adheres to when working or traveling. Clip his lead on and take a leisurely stroll around the area. Give him ample time to take in all the new sights and smells.

Being familiar with his surroundings will help your dog determine what is natural to the area and will help him to settle down in his new environment.

If your dog is a female and in season, I suggest you find a different time to go camping. Wild canines are attracted to her and will often boldly approach your campsite at night. Male dogs from nearby campsites will also be attracted. Try to plan ahead and avoid these times. You'll be glad you did!

Vacations longer than a weekend require a great deal more thought and planning. Especially backpacks. A backpack can only be as many days as you have food and supplies. The longest backpack I've done without coming out of the wilderness for supplies is seventeen days. This was without dogs. My friend and I were able to go that length of time because we had to catch fish every other day for food. Since I'm a firm believer in dogs not eating people food, a trip of this duration would be impossible without coming out for additional food or supplies.

Gather your dog's supplies and figure out how much he'll need to eat on a vigorous trip each day. I always like to bring an extra days food just in case it takes longer to get back.

If your dog's equipment weighs 6 lbs. and she eats one pound of food every day and your trip is eight days you're at 14 lbs. Add one extra day, and you have a total of 15lbs. This is equal to 25% of the weight of a 60 lb. Dog, which is a safe amount of weight for a dog that has been trained and has built up to carrying a heavy pack.

Your dogs size, age and activity level will determine how much he will need to eat every day, and how much equipment hc carrics. Seventeen days would never work out.

Changing your dogs diet on a trip is inadvisable. Even changing dry dog food requires that you slowly blend in the new food in his diet. Instantly changing it will most likely upset his stomach. Adding food gathered or caught in order to extend your trip is almost guaranteed to cause stomach problems. It's much safer to go for the period of time that works out safely.

Of course if you are car camping, or have the ability to get to stores that have your dogs food, then you can go for as long as time will allow.

Finding the same dog food as you normally use can be very difficult. Typically, we are camping in more remote areas than where we live. I like to use high quality dog foods and these are not found in grocery stores in big cities, much less small towns. I always measure out my dog's meals ahead of time and put each day's meal or meals in zip-lock bags and mark them with "Day One" or 1A and 1B and 2A and 2B if he eats twice a day. This way I know I've brought enough food and I don't have to remember if I've fed him or not. Most trips involve more activity for your dog than when he is at home, so I add the proper amount and always bring enough for an extra day or two in case you end up coming back a little later than planned.

I've always believed that eating once every twenty-four hours was too long in-between meals. Especially for an active dog. Once my dogs were of adult age, I switched the morning meal to a large milkbone or two and then gave them their regular dinner in the evening.

A milkbone in the morning is a nice and easy light breakfast for your dog. Food is energy, but going for a hike or any heavy activity right after a big meal can cause bloat in your dog. Bloat is a condition where the stomach can twist upon itself and become blocked. This is very serious and can possibly lead to death.

A typical morning when camping is coffee and some kind of a light breakfast for me and water and a milkbone for my dog. By the time camp is secure and we've stretched and cleaned up, the food has been digested and we are ready for the day's activities.

When going on long hiking trips, be sure and take many rest stops where packs are removed and water is offered. When the pack is off, your dog is more into a rest or break time attitude. This is also a good time to check for ticks and to check his pads. This needs to become routine or it will be too easily forgotten. At the end of the day we are often too tired to think about all the necessary checks and maintenance.

If his pads look like they are showing some signs of overuse or abuse don't hesitate to put his booties on right away. Worn and torn pads do not heal in a day or two.

After a few days of camping or backpacking your routine starts to become the days normal activities. Your dog has settled into his new environment and has got used to the sounds and smells that were so unfamiliar at first. Your camp, wherever it may be, starts becoming "home". This is when the trip really becomes the experience that allows true peace and harmony with your surroundings. As the days go by, you and your dog become used to the daily agenda, which lends itself to a more relaxed and less anxious attitude. Long trips allow your relation-ship to grow as you adapt to the new lifestyle together. Your dog will sense the more relaxed feelings you have and that helps him to settle in as well. These trips do a great deal to increase the bond between you. It gives both of you the opportunity to observe the other in a relaxed and more natural atmosphere.

It's hard to say exactly what kind of memo-ries a dog takes with him, but each trip seems to make a difference. Your dog learns to trust you in a whole new set of circum-stances and see what you are like without the daily stress of home life. You get to see your dog in a more natural environment and ap-preciate his incredible built-in abilities, which rarely get tapped at home.

Long trips can do more for mental and physical health than any therapist or exercise facility will ever achieve.

Chapter 12

FINAL THOUGHTS

There is nothing quite like taking a veteran dog on a camping or a backpacking trip. From the moment you start dragging out your camping supplies, he's anxiously anticipating spending quality time with you in an environment that was once his natural habitat.

Wherever we set our tent is home. After many miles and many trips, he learns your pace and what you expect of him when you stop or venture into difficult terrain. He's watching your every move for any indication of what you may want from him, be it in the form of hand signals, voice, or body language.

As we rest at our campsite, enjoying the peace and calm, our dogs become an extension of our ears and eyes. They never seem to be in such a deep sleep that any unusual sound or smell will not wake them. With trust in our devoted companion we can shut off some of our senses and further explore others.

We marvel at the abilities our dogs have. They rarely get a chance to fully use them at home. I began this book explaining how domesticated dogs have become. People have certainly distanced themselves from nature far more than domestic dogs. A canines' abilities to see in darkness, their acute hearing and incredible sense of smell are like that of a super being.

Our amazing and dedicated friend humbles us. We now achieve harmony. We no longer feel superiority. There is much to be learned from our dogs whose willingness and devotion is unparalleled in our world.

The Beginning

BONUS CHAPTER*
A SKUNK FORMULA THAT WORKS!

Poor puppy! Only trying to be friendly to the little kitty with the white stripe.

Well most skunks don't want to be friends, and they let you know about it in the most emphatic way.

Of course the rejected dog comes to you for solace ugh! What to do?

While most of us have heard of the tomato juice bath, and some have even tried it, it doesn't work, unless you want a red dog that smells like skunk and tomato juice. Nor does lemon juice, mayonnaise, peanut butter, or any other folk remedy you may have heard of.

HOW ABOUT SOME CHEMISTRY?

The molecules that cause the problem in skunk spray are called thiols, the same molecules that give rotten eggs their smell. Thiols are slightly acidic and are not very water soluble, which makes them very difficult to remove from such things as animal fur.

The problem is that simply washing them away doesn't work, even with the concoctions listed above. Even a tiny amount of thiols are very powerful and some will always remain. The trick is to neutralize them, and oxygen is the answer. It oxidizes the thiols in a chemical process where the oxygen is added to the sulfur atoms of the thiols. The thiols are converted chemically to molecules like sulfones and sulfoxides which are not only odorless, but also more water soluble.

This makes the skunk spray easier to wash off, but more importantly, any thiols that remain are no longer smelly!

What we need then, is a little oxygen generator.

HYDROGEN PEROXIDE TO THE RESCUE

The following mixture will produce all the oxygen necessary.

Ingredients:

1 qt. 3% Hydrogen Peroxide

1/4 cup Baking Soda

1 tsp. Dish Soap

Wet the dog. Mix the hydrogen peroxide, baking soda and dish soap together and apply liberally to the skunked areas of the dog. The front of the dog, (head and chest) will be the most likely area hit. Be careful not to get the mixture into the dog's eyes, nose or ears. Leave the mixture on the dog for five to ten minutes, then rinse several times. Bathe the dog normally after the treatment.

There is only one slight inconvenience: this recipe cannot be mixed ahead of time. When mixed, it effervesces and creates pressure. A capped bottle of this stuff will turn into a weapon of mass leakage and might even explode.

Also, be aware that the peroxide may bleach the dog's fur. This will cause no lasting problem, but your dog may have to put up with other dogs pointing and laughing!

DON'T THROW THAT TOMATO JUICE AWAY!

Now you can use it for it's intended purpose.

- ✔ Tomato Juice
- ✔ Gin
- ✔ Worchester Sauce
- ✔ Celery Salt
- ✔ Celery Stalk

After you are done dealing with your dog's unwelcome misadventure, mix these ingredients in the proportion of your choice and apply liberally to the lips, mouth, throat and stomach. Yours of course!

Credit for this remedy goes to chemist, Paul Krebaum, of Molex Inc. in Lisle, Illinois.

Thanks, Paul

*contributed by Michael Grant

ORDER MORE BOOKS !!!

Dogs On The Trail can be ordered directly from the publisher via our web page:

www.dogsonthetrail.com

or ask your local bookstore.

Quantity discounts are available from InsightOut Publishing for your hiking club, dog club or specialty store.
Visit us on the web at:

www.insightoutpublishing.com

We look forward to hearing from you.

Happy Trails!

Printed in the United States
49481LVS00003B/81

9 780976 994305